Sightseeing

A SPACE PANORAMA

Sightseeing

A SPACE PANORAMA

84 photographs from the NASA archives
selected by Barbara Hitchcock

With a Foreword by
Arthur C. Clarke

ALFRED A. KNOPF NEW YORK 1985

THIS IS A BORZOI BOOK
PUBLISHED BY ALFRED A. KNOPF, INC.

Copyright © 1985 by International Transactions, Inc.
Foreword copyright © 1985 by Serendib, B.V.
All rights reserved under International and Pan-American
Copyright Conventions.
Published in the United States by Alfred A. Knopf, Inc., New York, and
simultaneously in Canada by Random House of Canada Limited, Toronto.
Distributed by Random House, Inc., New York.
All photographs in *Sightseeing: A Space Panorama* were taken by
astronauts of the United States of America and are reproduced courtesy
of The National Aeronautics and Space Administration.
Library of Congress Cataloging in Publication Data
Riva, Peter
Sightseeing : a space panorama.
Catalog of an exhibition held at the National Air and Space Museum,
September 5–November 7, 1985.
1. Space photography—Exhibitions. I. Hitchcock, Barbara.
II. National Air and Space Museum. III. Title.
TR713.R58 1985   779'.96294   85-40347
ISBN 0-394-54243-6

Manufactured in Italy
FIRST EDITION

Acknowledgments

It is with sincere thanks that we wish to acknowledge the following:
James Ragan and Ron Gerlach of NASA (JSC), without whose identical vision this project would not have been possible.
Charles Biggs and James Morrison of NASA (JSC and Washington respectively), who proved that mountains can be moved, often.
Tom Winston of Technicolor Labs (NASA, JSC), devoted and knowledgeable librarian for all NASA's prime archive.
Brewster Shaw, astronaut (NASA, JSC), for his tacit support and open pleasure at seeing and being "on show" at the first exhibition in France.
Ernst Wildi (Hasselblad), for his infectious enthusiasm.
Victoria Wilson (Knopf), for proving, yet again, how important a great editor can be.
Lucien Clergue (artist, France), who was of vital assistance and enlisted the help of Groupe 7 and Maison Phénix of Paris.
Doug Ward and Ken Pederson, who both kept the wheels turning at NASA, perhaps at a speed that was "over the limit."
Eelco Wolf and the Polaroid Corporation, for providing Barbara with a flexible schedule to complete the long days at the light table in Houston.
Wendy Pollock (A.S.T.C., Washington, D.C.), a professional, always ready to work with a smile.
And, finally, Sandra Riva, without whose administration the *Sightseeing* project would have foundered.

The *Sightseeing* exhibition tour is arranged courtesy of the Association of Science-Technology Centers, Washington, D.C. The exhibition was underwritten by Victor Hasselblad Inc. The prints for the *Sightseeing* exhibition were printed by David Travis of Elmi Graphics, Hollywood, California.

The images in this book were taken with the following equipment:
Hasselblad: 500c, Superwide, ELM, Lunar Data Surface with lenses: Distagon 50-mm, Biogon 38-mm, Biogon 60-mm, Planar 80-mm, Planar 100-mm, Sonnar Superachromat 250-mm.
Linhof: Pantechnica.
All film stock was by Kodak.

Produced in cooperation with the Rencontres Internationales de la Photographie, Arles, France.

Foreword

Only twice in the history of mankind has a new window been opened on the universe, to reveal new worlds beyond all previous imagination. We have been lucky enough to live in the second such age.

The first began in 1609, when Galileo pointed his newly invented telescope at the heavens. He saw what no one before him had ever witnessed—the mountains of the Moon, the satellites of Jupiter, the densely packed star-clouds of the Milky Way—and, though he did not realize it, the rings of Saturn.

The second age of astronomical exploration had no such dramatic opening; we may date its beginnings from the early 1950s, when the first rocket-borne cameras were carried above the atmosphere. Incredible though this now seems, many were slow to realize the potential of images from space. In the early days of the Gemini program, I can recall trying to convince a skeptical NASA administration that it was essential to put a TV camera aboard the spacecraft.

The distinguished British astronomer Sir Fred Hoyle was one of the first to recognize the impact of views from space. In his 1950 book, *The Nature of the Universe,* he predicted that there would be a profound change in human attitudes when we could see photographs of our entire planet.

A dramatic proof of that occurred during the CBS coverage of the Apollo program, when Walter Cronkite was interviewing former President Lyndon Johnson. LBJ recalled that he sent copies of the famous Apollo 8 photo of the Earth hanging above the bleak lunar landscape to every head of state. He then reached into his pocket and produced, with obvious pride, the personal letter of thanks sent back by President Ho Chi Minh himself—at the very height of the Vietnam war. One might regard this as a tacit admission of the fact that there is only one family of man on this tiny planet, and that there are no frontiers visible from space.*

From the purely practical point of view, the images of Earth (whether by camera, LANDSAT scanners, or spaceborne radar) are certainly the most valuable, as may be proved by the fact that oil companies and similar organizations have paid millions of dollars for them. But the most mind-stretching are those of other worlds, starting with the Moon. In chronological order, here is my own short list of the images, which, by becoming part of our mental heritage, now sunder us irrevocably from all earlier generations.

---

*This is not strictly true. Some national boundaries are clearly visible, because of differing agricultural and irrigation practices in adjacent countries.

Orbiter: view across Copernicus crater

Apollo 8: Earth above lunar horizon

Apollo 11: astronaut on Moon

Viking: Martian landscape

Voyager: Jupiter, with satellites in transit

Voyager: the volcanoes of Io

Voyager: the rings of Saturn

What marvels will the future hold, comparable to these?

Well, before the end of this decade two more windows should be opening. The space telescope will increase tenfold our reach into the cosmos, besides giving far better definition of the stars and galaxies we can already observe. And closer to home—only a few billion kilometers away!—the Galileo spacecraft will begin the first detailed exploration of the moons of Jupiter.

As past history has shown, Nature is infinitely surprising; we can be sure that she has, as yet, revealed only a fraction of her wonders. To paraphrase Haldane's famous remark: The universe is not only stranger than we imagine—it is stranger than we *can* imagine....

Awesome and beautiful though they are, the pictures in this book are only a first installment, in a series that may go on forever.

ARTHUR C. CLARKE
Colombo, Sri Lanka

Preface

Several years ago, I noticed that although the images we were seeing from space were technically interesting, they were without emotional content. I could not understand, listening to the enthusiastic reports of the astronauts, how they could not have taken pictures that matched their excited descriptions of the beauty and thrill of space travel. With all the equipment and technology in the world (and beyond) at their disposal, why hadn't the astronauts taken pictures in the same way a tourist does, to show the folks back home what a great trip they'd had?

Through a chance meeting with James Ragan, a manager of NASA's Optics Division, who was responsible for developing the Nikon and Hasselblad NASA photographic systems, and Ron Gerlach, director of the Optics Division, it became clear that the astronauts had indeed taken many more images than we had been privileged to see—at least 150,000 more! From the beginning of the space program, the cameras taken into space were used to measure man and machine, not as a descriptive tool. The scientific structure of the space program, purposely devoid of emotion and subjectivity, prevented aesthetic evaluation of the astronauts' personal pictures. In addition, NASA was often slow in delivering the film to the press; when photos finally arrived at editorial offices, they were already "old news," and thus never published in newspapers and magazines.

Using the most exacting curatorial procedures, Barbara Hitchcock reviewed every roll of film in the Johnson Space Center's Astronaut Library of handheld still images, searching for those images whose aesthetic content could make us better able to grasp the reality of space. The photographs she found, eighty-four reproduced here and included in the *Sightseeing* exhibition, which is touring the country, astound, thrill and convey the visceral joy of space travel.

Man is, after all, the only explorer on this planet. And traditionally man has used art to express and translate the new experience for those left behind. The cave drawings in France depict hairy cows seen in a far-off valley; the watercolors by Captain Cook's first officer on his expedition to the Hawaiian Islands showed strange animals and people; the early Egyptians upon discovering sheep on a trek into Asia drew them as fluffy goats. Such artwork, found around the world throughout history, is no more than an attempt to describe new experiences, new places, new frontiers. And, without it, who would have followed Columbus, Cook, or da Gama? Those who came after realized that a new visual language and understanding were necessary to appreciate—and, in fact, to exist in—the uncharted territory.

One is lost as an astronaut tries to describe his visions and feelings, that which is literally beyond our terrestrial experience. Using the best tools of this (their) day, the astronauts have taken extraordinary images of their experiences in this new frontier, and in viewing them we might remember those moments and places in history when similar travel pictures were first shown: Admiralty House in London, as Captain Cook's watercolors were displayed to amazement and great excitement; the Cardinal's tribunal in Venice, as an illustrator worked to capture Marco Polo's descriptions; Pharaoh Rameses viewing the illustrations of his expeditions' discoveries in Nubia; a tribe gathering around the painter as he added to the cave wall drawings after a scouting trip.

Recently a shuttle crew gathered around a light table in a darkened room after returning from eight days in orbit and, looking at the pictures they had taken, were enthralled as the images conjured up sensations of their journey. I was reminded of a slide show my wife and I gave for friends after our recent stay in Switzerland; the beauty in the pictures caused a guest to exclaim, "I wish we'd been there!"

The pictures in *Sightseeing* should be experienced as a way to participate in man's new reality on the frontiers of space. These new "cave drawings" are crucial to our understanding of new experiences that wait just over the horizon, beyond Earth's atmosphere.

PETER RIVA
Exhibition Coordinator

The eighty-four photographs in this volume were selected on the basis of earth-bound conventions: admiration for dramatic lighting, form, color, textures, emotion, and intensity of vision—for a gesture captured, for a universality, for a detail or perspective never before seen.

If photography had not yet existed, it would have been necessary to invent it, to provide evidence that space flight is more than technology alone. And it is that quality that makes these images unique. Where humans go, art goes also.

The first flight, the first Moon landing, the first space walk were the accomplishments of many. In these pictures we can recall that original "space-emotion" in 1969, that sharing, that feeling of union and of belonging to our planet. I'd like to dedicate this volume to all who shared—or wish they had shared—that moment.

BARBARA PERITZ HITCHCOCK

Sightseeing

A SPACE PANORAMA

The first untethered space walk, on February 7, 1984. Bruce McCandless II, a mission specialist, wears a 300-pound Manned Maneuvering Unit (MMU) with 24 nitrogen gas thrusters and a 35mm camera. The MMU enabled him to travel 140 feet away from the shuttle Challenger.
Shuttle Mission 41b, February 3 to 11, 1984

The Grand Erg Oriental dune range in Algeria, taken from the shuttle Challenger.
Shuttle Mission 41b, February 3 to 11, 1984

A solar panel used to convert sunlight into electricity—part of the floating space station Skylab. The round disc houses the Apollo Telescope Mount, which enabled astronauts to photograph the Sun, stars, and other astral bodies. In the background, the Earth. Skylab Mission 3, July 28 to September 25, 1973

Astronaut Donald Peterson, on a 50-foot tether line during his 4-hour, 3-orbit space walk,
traveling toward the tail of the shuttle Challenger as it glides around the Earth.
Shuttle Mission 6, April 4 to 9, 1983

Mozambique, the Zambezi River delta. Note the trailing clouds from bush fires.
Apollo Mission 7, October 11 to 22, 1968

9

The mauve coast of Australia passes beneath the wing of the shuttle
Columbia as it orbits at 17,500 miles per hour.
Shuttle Mission 5, November 11 to 16, 1982

The first Extra Vehicular Activity (EVA) by Edward H. White II, on June 3, 1965. During his
space walk, which lasted 23 minutes, White passed over the United States and the South Atlantic
tethered by an umbilical cord (note black stowage bag), which the astronauts called "the snake."
White to James McDivitt (who took this photograph): "I was sorry to see it draw to a close…
I was reluctant to come in…."   Gemini Mission IV, June 3 to 7, 1965

The Canadian Remote Manipulator Arm being tested during
Columbia's second flight. Note the elbow-mounted video camera.
Shuttle Mission 2, November 12 to 14, 1981

India, the Great Himalayas.
Shuttle Mission 1, April 12 to 14, 1981

Argentina, the Rio Calchaquí in the Sierra de Aguas Calientes.
Shuttle Mission 41b, Challenger, February 3 to 11, 1984

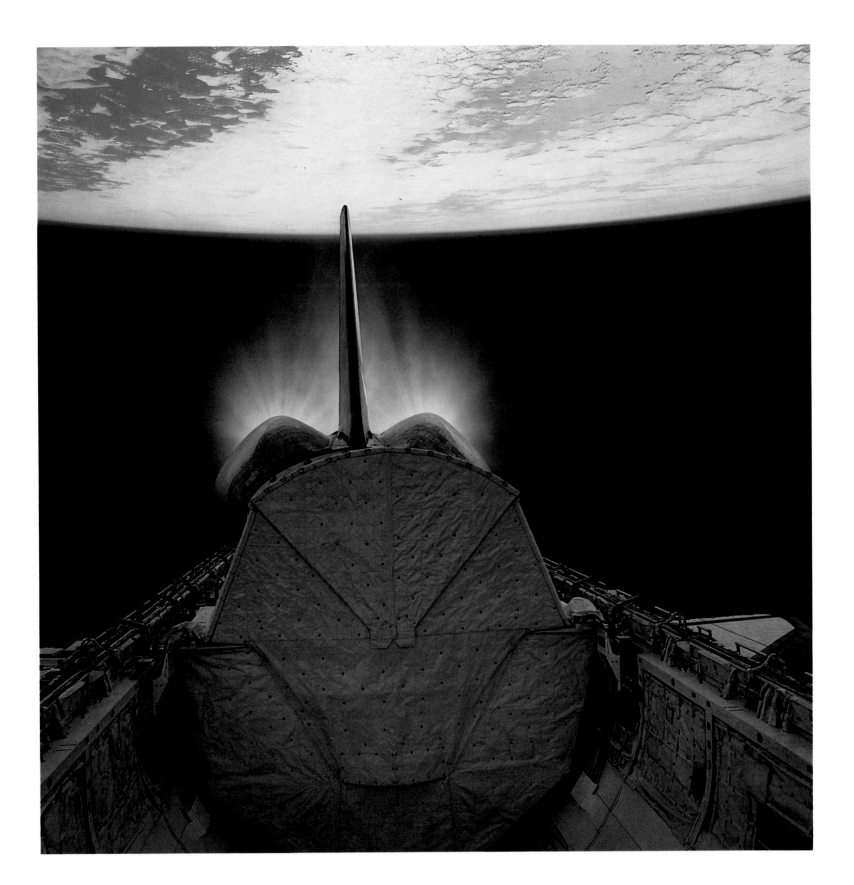

Columbia's thrusters are fired in preparation for the first launch of a satellite from the shuttle. The satellite is housed in the cargo pallet with the clam doors.   Shuttle Mission 5, November 11 to 16, 1982

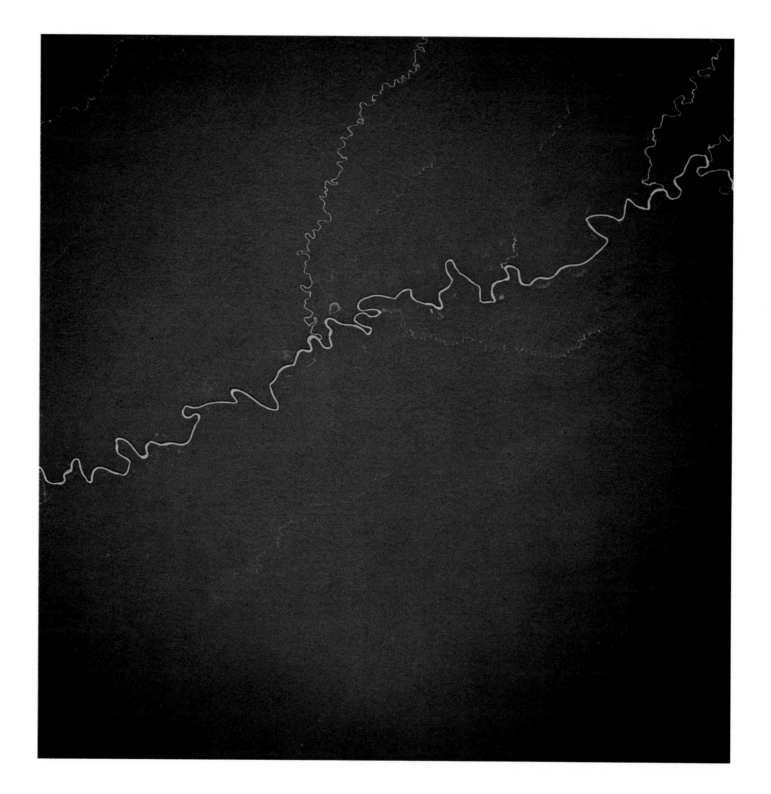

Seen from a low orbit (150 miles), the Amazon Jungle with the River Envira.
Apollo-Soyuz Test Project, July 15 to 24, 1975

Saudi Arabia, the Nafūd Desert, taken with the first 4-x-5-inch camera in space.
Shuttle Mission 41c, April 6 to 13, 1984

Chatham and Pitt Islands off New Zealand with cumulus cloud streaks.
Skylab Mission 4, November 16, 1973 to February 8, 1974

Mauritania's El Djouf desert with Richat structure.
Gemini Mission XII, November 11 to 15, 1966

Russian spacecraft Soyuz in low orbit. Its spherical shape is a result of the
Soviet's use of nitrogen/oxygen instead of the pure oxygen atmosphere used
in U.S. spacecraft at that time.   Apollo-Soyuz Test Project, July 15 to 24, 1975

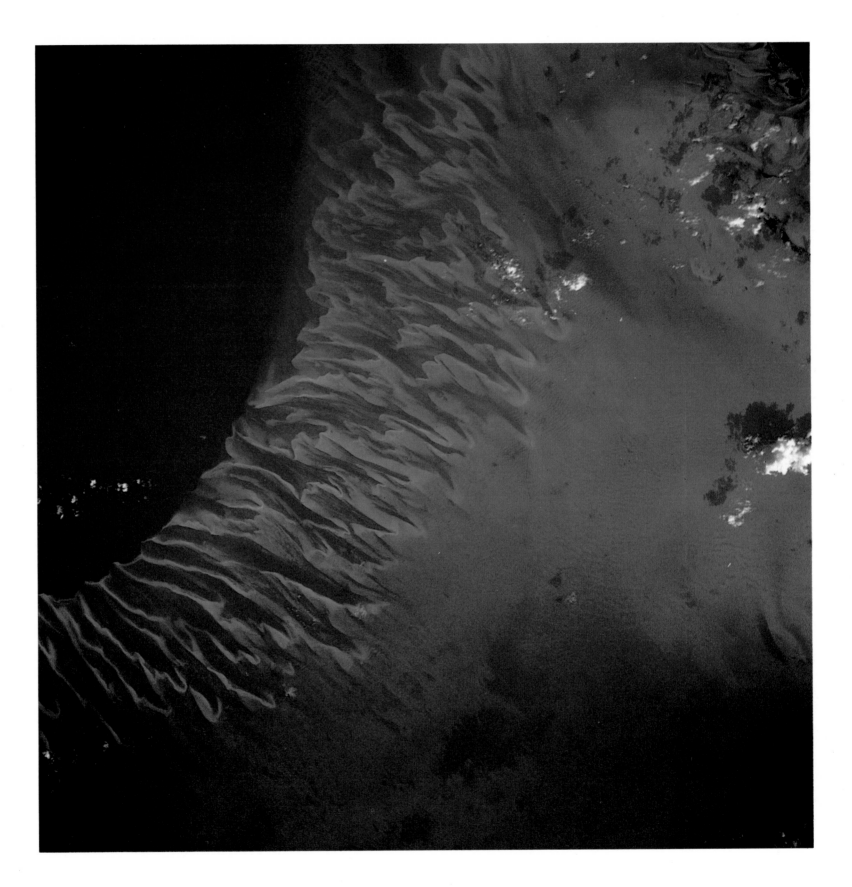

Taken from Columbia's first operational flight over the Bahamas. Looking through
the water you see the sand patterns on the ocean floor, caused by strong currents.
Shuttle Mission 5, November 11 to 16, 1982

The North Gulf of Aden showing Somalia, Oman, and Yemen.
Shuttle Mission 41c, April 6 to 13, 1984

Ed White, during the first U.S. space walk: "There's no difficulty in recontacting the spacecraft…
particularly as long as you move nice and slow…." The chest pack controls the coolant and
oxygen systems. The reflection in White's visor shows the open door of the Gemini spacecraft
and astronaut James McDivitt taking the photograph. Communication from Cape Canaveral
(CapCom): "The flight director says 'get back in!'" White: "Back in?!" McDivitt: "Back in!…"
Gemini Mission IV, June 3 to 7, 1965

Astronaut Owen Garriott, standing on the outside of Skylab, retrieves film from the solar camera for measuring Sun flares and other solar phenomena. Garriott holds the record for the single longest EVA (Extra Vehicular Activity) at 13 hours, 42 minutes. The Skylab orbited at 14,000 miles per hour, 260 miles above the Earth.   Skylab Mission 3, July 28 to September 25, 1973

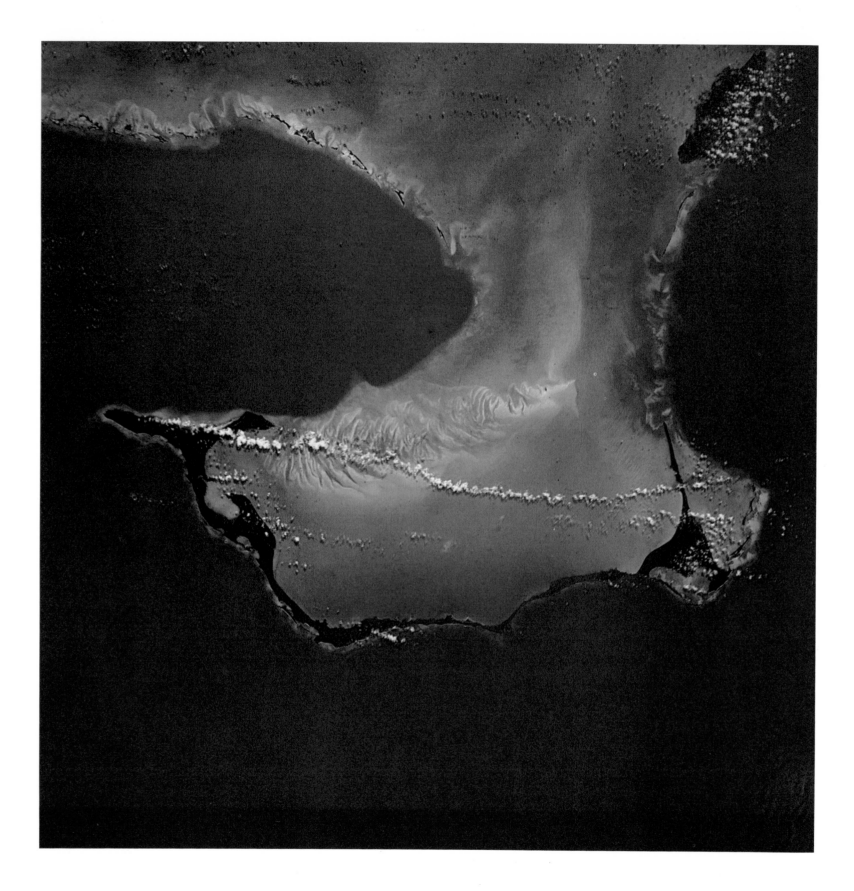

The Bahamas seen from Challenger.
Shuttle Mission 6, April 4 to 9, 1983

A South Pacific coral atoll drifts by at 18,000 miles per hour.
Shuttle Mission 41b, February 3 to 11, 1984

Pakistan and the Sulaimān Range seen during the second test flight of Columbia.
Shuttle Mission 2, November 12 to 14, 1981

As Skylab Mission 3 departs following a 59-day, 25-million-mile voyage, the crew of astronauts, Alan Bean, Owen Garriott, and Jack Lousma, took this photograph of the Apollo Telescope Mount, with the 4 Solar Array wings and, below, the Multiple Docking Adapter into which their Command and Service Module (CSM) was docked. The Skylab, which weighed 200,000 pounds and was 120 feet long and 30 feet in diameter, later fell to Earth.

Skylab Mission 3, July 28 to September 25, 1973

During the Apollo 9 10-day mission, the first docking of the CSM and LM (Lunar Module), astronaut Russell "Rusty" Schweickart stands in the doorway of the LM, with Hasselblad in hand, wearing the new Apollo EVA suit with self-contained life support systems. In his visor are reflected the Earth and the CSM with hatch open, showing astronaut David Scott taking his picture.
Apollo Mission 9, March 3 to 13, 1969

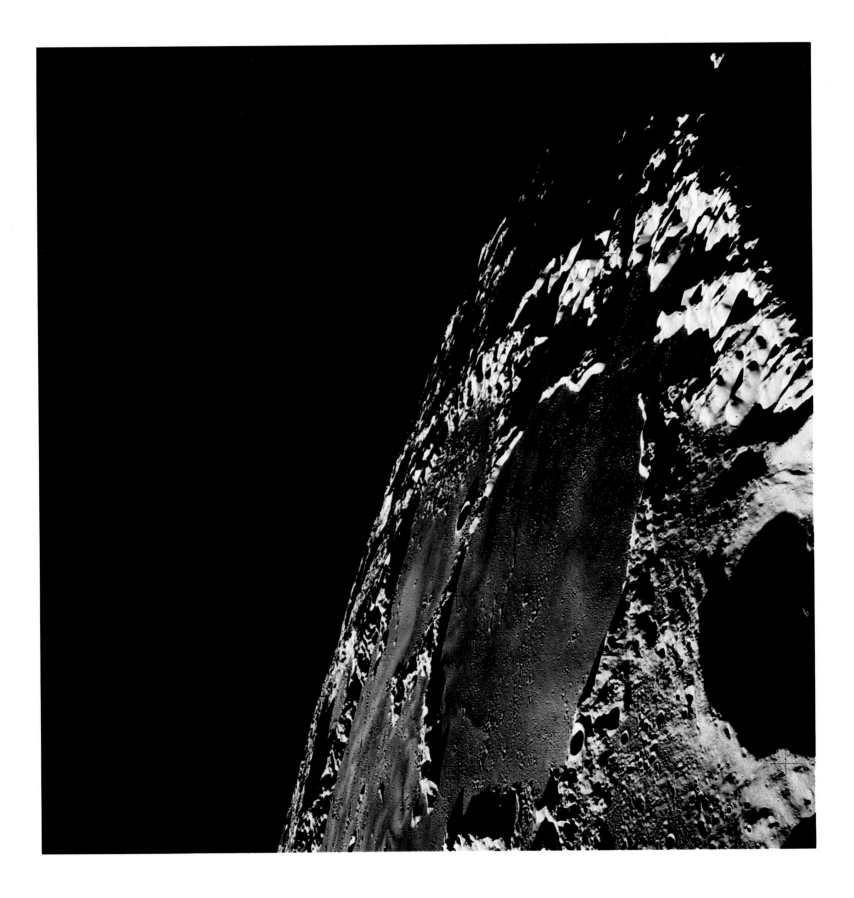

The Moon photographed from the orbiting CSM Endeavor by astronaut Al Worden.
Apollo Mission 15, July 26 to August 7, 1971

The Moon, taken from the CSM Yankee Clipper, 50 miles up in lunar orbit.
The craters are 250 miles wide.   Apollo Mission 12, November 14 to 24, 1969

The Moon. A view of the boulder-strewn area of Taurus-Littrow during the last
Apollo and lunar mission.   Apollo Mission 17, December 7 to 19, 1972

Astronaut James Irwin loading samples onto the Lunar Rover (LRV). The Lunar Rover was stored
unassembled on the side of the Lunar Module and had to be assembled on the Moon.
Apollo Mission 15, July 26 to August 7, 1971

37

A view of crescent Earth 250,000 miles away from the surface of the Moon.
Apollo Mission 15, July 26 to August 7, 1971

Astronaut Harrison "Jack" Schmitt holding experiment equipment. Above him, the Earth.
Apollo Mission 17, December 7 to 19, 1972

Jack Schmitt, standing by a large boulder at the foothills of the Moon's north massif, with
the Lunar Rover. On the LRV is a disc antenna and, on the front bumper, a remote-controlled
(by Houston Space Center) video camera.   Apollo Mission 17, December 7 to 19, 1972

Alan Shepard and Edgar Mitchell's Lunar Module Antares.
Apollo Mission 14, January 31 to February 9, 1971

The Earth rising over Monumental Rock on Taurus-Littrow.
Apollo Mission 17, December 7 to 19, 1972

Shadowed self-portrait, Taurus-Littrow.
Apollo Mission 17, December 7 to 19, 1972

Buzz Aldrin, holding on to the outside of the Gemini spacecraft, has just completed his
second space walk (duration 2 hours and 8 minutes). He made three EVAs in all.
Gemini Mission XII, November 11 to 15, 1966

Sunset taken at an altitude of 400 miles on the first Apollo manned flight.
Apollo Mission 7, October 11 to 22, 1968

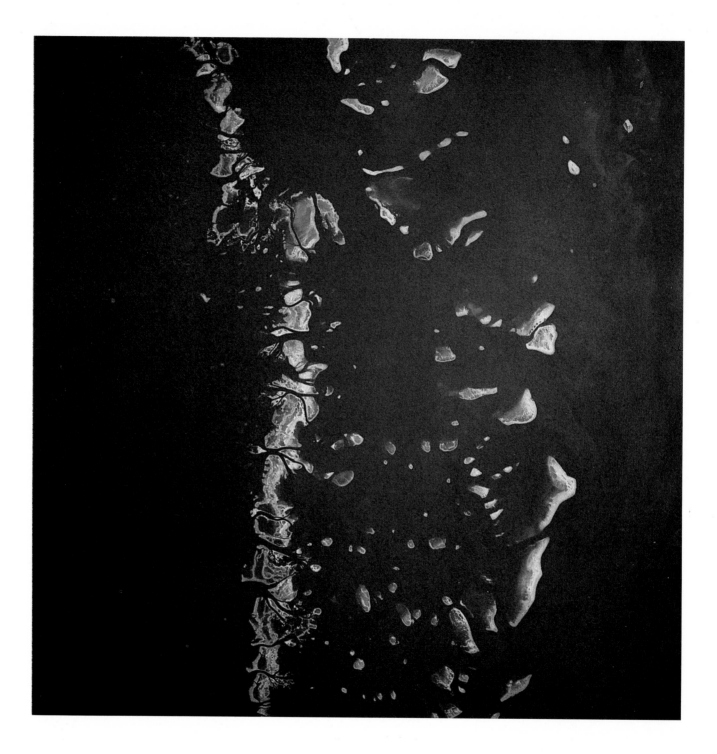

The Great Barrier Reef of Australia seen from Challenger on its third mission.
Shuttle Mission 8, August 30 to September 5, 1983

Australia's Cape Melville, Queensland, and the Great Barrier Reef.
Apollo Mission 7, October 11 to 22, 1968

The Soviet Union, Sakhalin Island with ice packs breaking up in the Tatar Strait.
Skylab Mission 2, May 25 to June 22, 1973

Shuttle Challenger orbits at 18,000 miles per hour, 200 miles above the Earth, as astronaut
Story Musgrave uses special latch tools while attached by cable in the open cargo bay.
Shuttle Mission 6, April 4 to 9, 1983

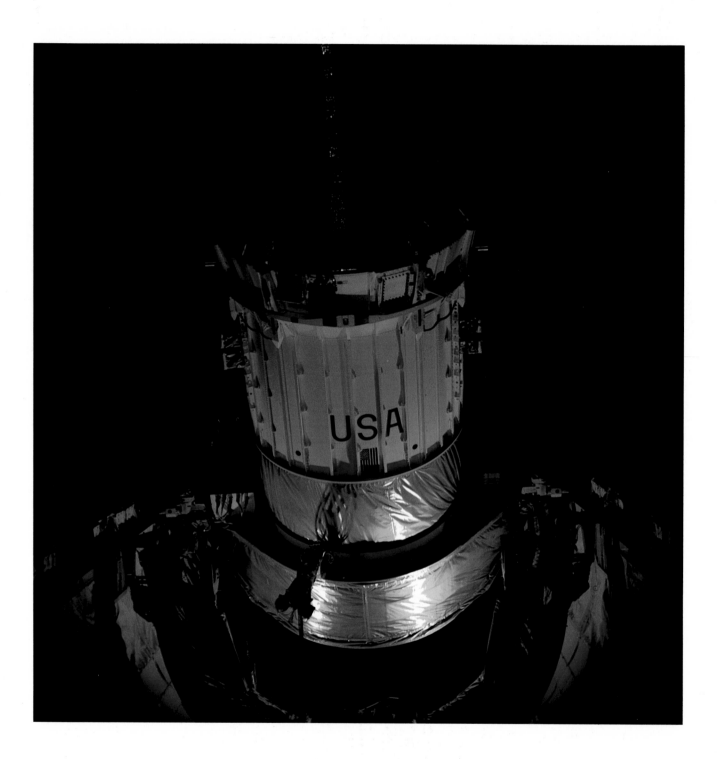

The Tracking-and-Data-Relay Satellite, ready for launch, sits in the open
cargo bay of Challenger.   Shuttle Mission 6, April 4 to 9, 1983

Columbia's tail glowing in the sunset. A sunset occurs every hour and 20 minutes as the
Columbia completes its orbit of the Earth.   Shuttle Mission 5, November 11 to 16, 1982

Africa's equatorial green shows clearly as the Apollo CSM and LM leave Earth
on the way to the first lunar landing.   Apollo Mission 11, July 16 to 24, 1969

Traveling at a speed that took the spacecraft from Los Angeles to New York in less than 10 minutes, astronaut Lovell sat in an open door and photographed this view of Gemini and the Earth passing below.   Gemini Mission XII, November 11 to 15, 1966

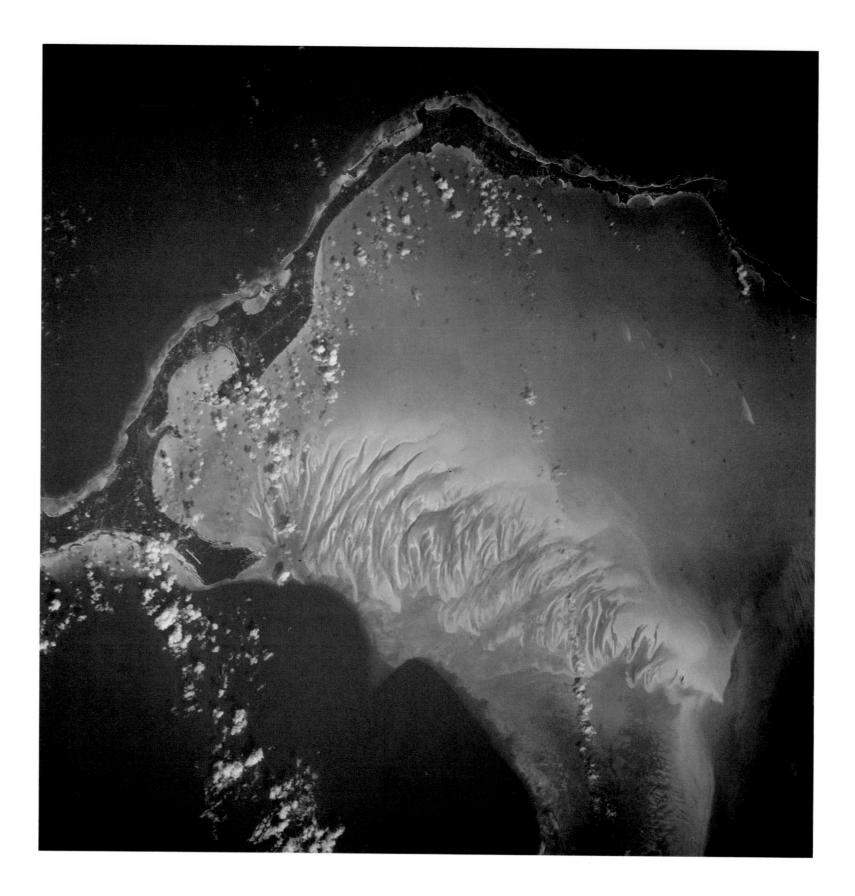

The Bahamas seen from the spacecraft Columbia on its maiden voyage.
Shuttle Mission 1, April 12 to 14, 1981

The Southern Zagros Mountains of Iran. The crater-like shapes are eroded salt domes.
Apollo Mission 7, October 11 to 22, 1968

Skylab, seen by Charles Conrad, Joseph Kerwin, and Paul Weitz on their return journey to Earth.
Note the golden parasol they erected over the scarred and burnt hull to reduce its internal
temperature from 125°F to 70°F.   Skylab Mission 2, May 25 to June 22, 1973

The scar-like diagonal rift terminating, at upper left, in Lake Mead is the Grand Canyon.
Skylab Mission 3, July 28 to September 25, 1973

Thunderhead clouds at sunset seen from Challenger on its first flight.
Shuttle Mission 6, April 4 to 9, 1983

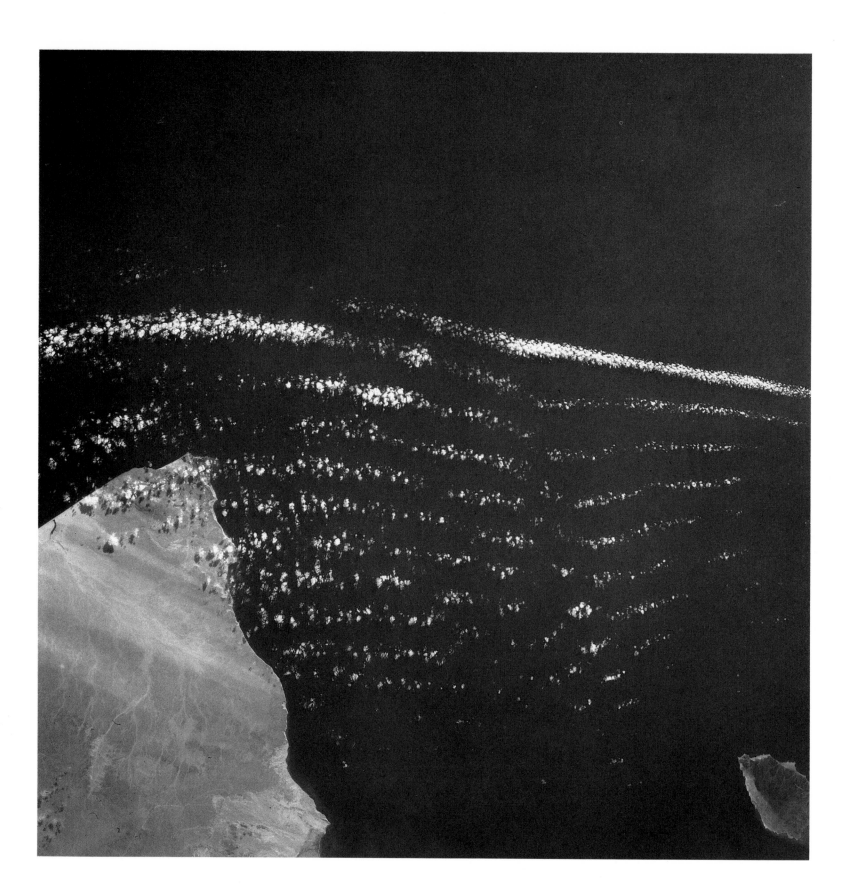

The Ra's al Madrakah region in Arabia, with transverse clouds, seen from Columbia
on its second test flight.   Shuttle Mission 2, November 12 to 14, 1981

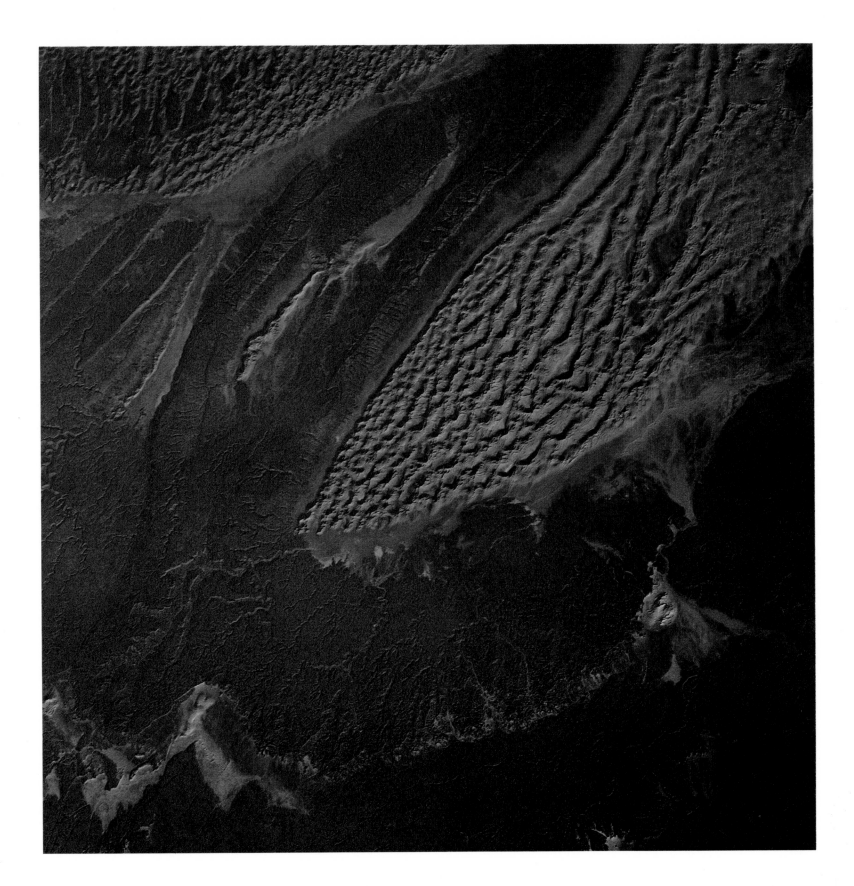

Algeria's star dune chains and flooded plain in the Grand Erg Oriental range.
Shuttle Mission 2, November 12 to 14, 1981

A full view of the shuttle Challenger. The golden cylinder is the Solar Max satellite, which has been
retrieved by the remote manipulator arm (at right). Shuttle Mission 41c, April 6 to 13, 1984

Algeria, the Marzūq Basin and sand dunes near the Ajjer Plateau at sunset, taken from Skylab on its last mission.   Skylab Mission 4, November 16, 1973 to February 8, 1974

The islands of Hawaii and Maui. At the center, the snowcapped Mauna Loa volcano.
Skylab Mission 4, November 16, 1973 to February 8, 1974

Seen from the Gemini spacecraft: the Ajena Docking Vehicle (ADV) orbiting as it awaits
rendezvous and docking. This photograph was taken by Michael Collins, who later piloted
the first moon-landing mission CSM.   Gemini Mission X, July 18 to 24, 1966

The Great Himalayas at sunrise.
Shuttle Mission 5, November 11 to 16, 1982

Astronaut James Lovell's photograph of Buzz Aldrin walking in space. Note the mission emblem on the right upper-arm pen pocket containing ballpoint pens.
Gemini Mission XII, November 11 to 15, 1966

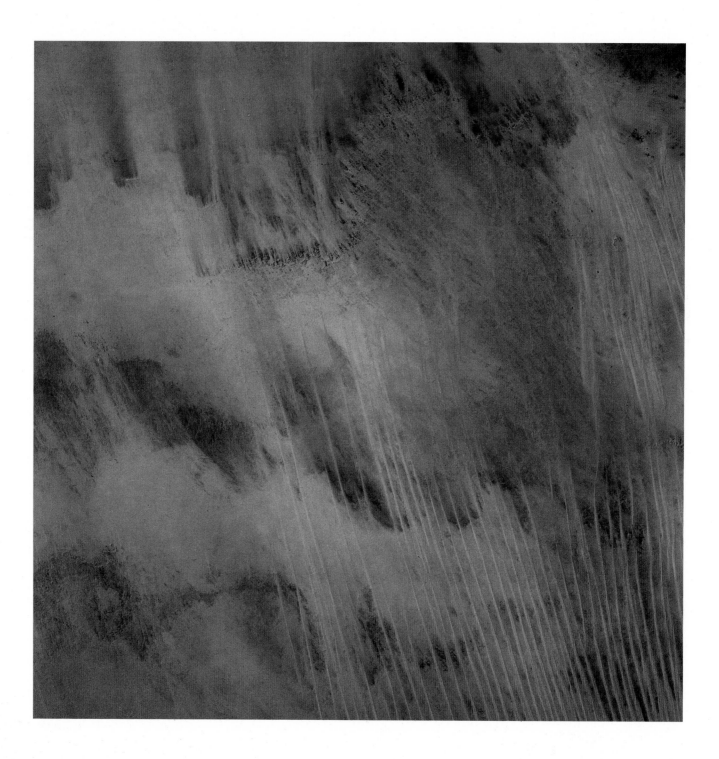

Egypt, the ranges of Abū Ballās and the Great Western Erg and longitudinal
dunes taken from Challenger.   Shuttle Mission 41c, April 6 to 13, 1984

The Bay of Imbituba of Brazil seen from Challenger.
Shuttle Mission 8, August 30 to September 5, 1983

The two crews of Gemini VI and Gemini VII (seen here from the former) rendezvoused for the first space meeting of two spacecraft.   Gemini Mission VI-A, December 15 and 16, 1965

Dr. Story Musgrave, a mission specialist, attaches an equipment container to the 50-foot cable on the side of the open cargo bay above the liquids containers. Behind him is the cradle for the Tracking-and-Data-Relay Satellite (TDRS-A) previously launched from Challenger.
Shuttle Mission 6, April 4 to 9, 1983

The Earth, 160 miles below, photographed by astronaut Thomas Stafford. Attached to the umbilical cord is astronaut Gene Cernan (out of view).   Gemini IX-A, June 3 to 6, 1966

The Nafūd Desert in Saudi Arabia as Challenger passes over it at 17,500 miles per hour.
Shuttle Mission 41c, April 6 to 13, 1984

The light area in the center of the picture is phytoplankton (microscopic marine organisms).
It is unusual to see this large a group bloom, since it is an annual event of short duration.
Skylab Mission 4, November 16, 1973 to February 8, 1974

Sunset over Egypt and the Sudan with Lake Nasser.
Apollo Mission 7, October 11 to 22, 1968

Columbia's tail dips toward Earth as it circles the planet at 18,000 miles per hour.
Shuttle Mission 5, November 11 to 16, 1982

Bruce McCandless, wearing the back-up Manned Maneuvering Unit complete with Trunnion Pin
Acquisition Device (TPAD), used for docking with another spacecraft or satellite, practices upside
down in the cargo bay of Challenger.   Shuttle Mission 41b, February 3 to 11, 1984

Brazil. The Cape of São Tomé showing sediment from the Amazon River and ancient shoreline. Taken with high contrast 4-x-5-inch film specially developed for the U.S. Navy.   Shuttle Mission 41c, April 6 to 13, 1984

Australia's Great Sandy Island and Bundaberg (top) in Queensland seen from Challenger's cockpit roof windows.   Shuttle Mission 8, August 30 to September 5, 1983

Ed White drifting during the first U.S. space walk.
Gemini Mission IV, June 3 to 7, 1965

Command Pilot Thomas Stafford looking out of his window of the Gemini
spacecraft. With barely enough room for the slightest physical movement,
each Gemini astronaut used his window and occasional EVAs to escape
confinement.   Gemini Mission IX-A, June 3 to 6, 1966

Algeria stretches below the Ajena Docking Vehicle and antenna.
Gemini Mission XI, September 12 to 15, 1966

The star dune chain and flooded plain in the Grand Erg Oriental range in Algeria,
taken from the Gemini spacecraft with Frank Borman and James Lovell.
Gemini Mission VII, December 4 to 18, 1965

The Sesayap River delta in Borneo.
Shuttle Mission 7, June 18 to 24, 1983

Jack Lousma standing in front of the Solar Array wing of Skylab during a space walk, with the
Earth and the golden repair parasol covering Skylab reflected in his visor. Note the extra-long
watchband to permit its being worn outside of his spacesuit.
Skylab Mission 3, July 28 to September 25, 1973

Skylab seen by the departing crew after 28 days in Earth orbit.
Skylab Mission 2, May 25 to June 22, 1973

With the U.S. flag on his left shoulder and the Earth reflected in his visor, Buzz Aldrin
clings to the Ajena Docking Vehicle during Extra Vehicular Activity experiments
on the last Gemini flight. Gemini Mission XII, November 11 to 15, 1966

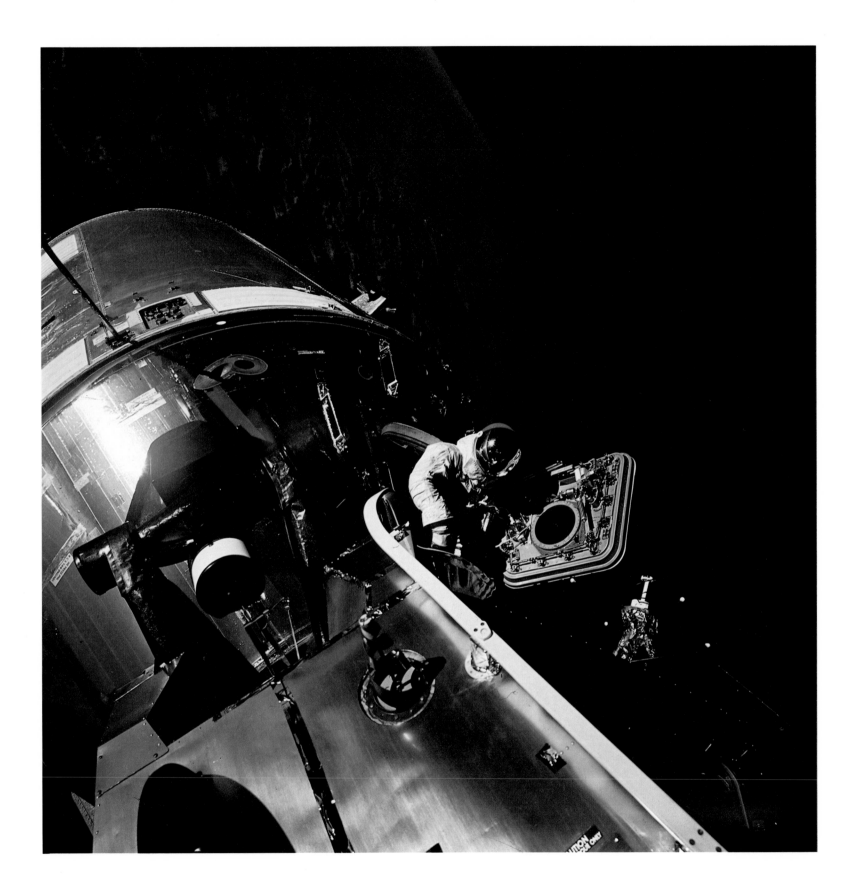

David Scott emerges from the hatch of the Apollo Command and Service Module
as it orbits the Earth while docked with the Lunar Module for the first time.
Apollo Mission 9, March 3 to 12, 1969

The Bahamas as seen by the crew of Challenger.
Shuttle Mission 6, April 4 to 9, 1983

The SPAS remote control camera looks down on the spaceship
Columbia set against thick cloud cover 200 hundred miles below.
Shuttle Mission 7, June 18 to 24, 1983

Ed White holding in his right hand a jet gun used to control his movements; the ship is reflected in his visor.   Gemini Mission IV, June 3 to 7, 1965

Ed White on the first U.S. space walk.
Gemini Mission IV, June 3 to 7, 1965

Tumbling and floating above the surface of the Earth, Ed White enjoyed 23 minutes
of EVA as he and his Gemini spacecraft sped from California to the South Atlantic.
Gemini Mission IV, June 3 to 7, 1965